THE GARDENS OF

# WAVE HILL

# The Gardens
## *of* WAVE HILL

PHOTOGRAPHY: MICK HALES
PROJECT DIRECTOR: SUZY BROWN
CONTRIBUTING EDITOR: SCOTT CANNING
EDITOR: ELIZABETH EDELSON
DESIGN: GRENFELL PRESS
PLANT RESEARCH: LAUREL RIMMER AND MARILYN YOUNG

*Wave Hill thanks Beverly Frank for making this publication possible.*
*Her heartfelt generosity and ongoing commitment to Wave Hill*
*are deeply appreciated by her colleagues on the Board of Directors*
*and by the entire Wave Hill community.*

DISTRIBUTED BY WAVE HILL
675 WEST 252ND STREET
BRONX, NEW YORK 10471-2899
TEL 718.549.3200  FAX 718.884.8952  WWW.WAVEHILL.ORG

For Marco Polo Stufano and John Nally,
*who created and nurtured the
original vision of Wave Hill
and crafted the landscape pictured in these pages.*

# The Gardens of
# WAVE HILL

IT IS OFTEN OBSERVED that Wave Hill is one of New York City's treasures. Its magnificent gardens, grounds, and vistas are unparalleled, and cherished by many city residents who find at Wave Hill an inviting and bountiful oasis of natural beauty. Wave Hill also enjoys international acclaim for its gardens, where the harmony of artistry and nature is made manifest. Their splendor is the outcome of a distinctive approach to horticulture that privileges plantsmanship, aesthetic sensibility, and the human experience of the natural environment. The resulting abundance is renowned for its intimacy of scale and its carefully cultivated serendipity: at Wave Hill, even the most seasoned gardeners can take joy in the unexpected.

Gardens and landscapes are canvases on which we explore our evolving relationships to nature. As a public garden and cultural center, Wave Hill is dedicated to fostering connections between people and the natural world. Every day, its resources serve as a living laboratory for the discovery, appreciation, and study of the natural environment through a wealth of educational programs and arts presentations. For this we owe very great thanks to Wave Hill's superb Board of Directors, who provide indispensable leadership and guidance, and to the

Perkins-Freeman family, who made the extraordinary gift of this estate to the City of New York in 1960 and continue their stewardship of this special place. And we are deeply grateful to the City of New York and its leadership, whose support of Wave Hill and our city's cultural institutions makes our operations possible.

If you have not yet visited Wave Hill, I hope it will soon have a chance to welcome you. In the meantime, these pages will introduce you to some of the gardens' more notable features. If you have enjoyed their glory in person, this book will help to illuminate some less visible aspects, like design strategies and cultivation regimens, while serving as a memento of Wave Hill throughout the seasons. We are most grateful to photographer Mick Hales for so beautifully capturing Wave Hill's tremendous variety, and to Brian R. Zipp for his generous support of Mick's work here. And we thank Beverly Frank, one of Wave Hill's staunchest supporters and dearest friends, who made this publication possible. Beverly's unstinting devotion to Wave Hill offers inspiration to Director of Horticulture Scott Canning and the Wave Hill Gardeners, whose plentiful talents sustain our living collections. She dedicates this book to Marco Polo Stufano and John Nally, artists and visionaries whose achievements continue to inspire wonder in all who visit Wave Hill.

KATE FRENCH
*President and Executive Director*

## Pergola Overlook

OVERLOOKING the spectacular vista of the Hudson River and Palisades, the Pergola at Wave Hill celebrates nature's drama and dynamism. Framing the bucolic expanse of the Great Lawn, the Pergola's arrangement of hanging baskets and containers is constantly changing, in direct response to the ever-shifting character of light and weather that is so perceptible in this breathtaking spot.

*The hardy kiwi vine* Actinidia arguta *clothes the structure in fresh green foliage, providing shade-loving plants and visitors with a cool respite from summer sunlight.*

*The Italianate stone structure is a striking stage
for inspired displays that focus on the form of
single plants and play with combinations.
Specimen plants in single containers are
interspersed with mixed containers, creating color
and interest to enhance the river view.*

*Flowering trees can be found throughout Wave Hill's grounds.* Cornus kousa (RIGHT) *frames a view of the Hudson below the pergola. A bed devoted to* Magnolia stellata *hybrids is a cloud of pastel color in April.*

## Marco Polo Stufano Conservatory

Tender plants from around the world are sheltered in the Marco Polo Stufano Conservatory complex: gardens under glass that honor Wave Hill's founding Director of Horticulture. The Palm House explodes with riotous color in winter months, yielding a dazzling display to stimulate the senses. Cacti and succulents fascinate with their infinite variety, and visitors to the Tropical House are enveloped in its incredible diversity of plants from warm climates.

*Inside the Palm House, trailing and scandent plants are shown off to their greatest advantage. The vivid, electric blue of* Pycnostachys dawei *blazes bright during winter days.*

*Vibrant South African bulbs cavort among*
*exotic foliage plants from around the world,*
*which provide the structural underpinnings*
*for an ever-changing overlay of color.*

*Hanging baskets create a sense of intimate enclosure.*

*The architecture of the Echeveria (RIGHT)*
*is remarkable year-round, and in winter it blushes*
*with pink, red, and maroon tones. As plants come*
*in and out of bloom during winter's cold,*
*compositions like the one below are changed often*
*—sometimes every few days—to highlight them at*
*their peak of perfection.*

## Alpine, Dry and Herb Gardens

THE STONE FOUNDATIONS of a former greenhouse reflect and retain the sun's warmth, and provide these connected garden areas with a strong frame. Narrow beds and paths invite close observation of remarkable plants. The alpine troughs and views of jewel-like specimens in the T.H. Everett Alpine House delight alpine plant enthusiasts from far and wide.

*Hardy alpines cascade down a rustic stone wall adjacent to the T.H. Everett Alpine House, which shelters more tender plants arranged to be viewed from outside.*

*In the Herb Garden, ornamental, culinary, and medicinal herbs from around the world make their home among bluestone paths.*

*Silver foliage predominates in the Dry Garden* (BELOW), *home to plants from arid climates that require sharp drainage and benefit from retained and reflected heat. A representative collection is artfully displayed in the Herb Garden* (RIGHT).

## Wild Garden

Wave Hill's Wild Garden is a glorious exercise in naturalistic gardening. The hillside site bursts with plants from around the world whose wild flower appearance gives a buoyant, planted-by-nature effect to the garden. Intensive cultivation is required to achieve this sense of abundant abandon: the yews, for instance, must be pruned one to two times each year to maintain their billowing, cloudlike forms. A rustic gazebo that has graced the site since at least 1915 provides an inviting, shady vantage point for river views. Artfully designed to celebrate nature's serendipitous beauty, in this pastoral garden the hand of the gardener is deliberately left unseen.

*An informal look is carefully maintained in the Wild Garden by featuring wild species and single flowers. The meandering path uses changing materials and elevations to guide a visitor's steps towards the most advantageous views.*

*A bench in this secluded corner devoted to Wave Hill's dear friend Netta Lockwood invites quiet reflection. The clematis mosaic remembers her favorite flower.*

*Fall is Wave Hill's peak season, when
the Wild Garden reveals autumnal foliage,
fruits, and flowers. Raucous color, like
the animated yellow of this Forsythia sage,
is all around.*

*Plants in the Wild Garden*
*self-sow most prolifically along*
*the edges of the gravel paths, and each*
*year some are left untouched.*

Juniperus
'N
Cupr

*Specimen trees are Wave Hill's grand monuments, a place of rest for eyes astonished by the profusion of detail found in the gardens.*

*In the second-growth forest of the Herbert*
*and Hyonja Abrons Woodland, visitors*
*can walk the shady trail.*

## Aquatic Garden and Monocot Garden

The elegant Aquatic Garden reaches its zenith in late July and August, just as many other garden plants begin to weary from the summer's heat. The pool is a refreshing oasis surrounded by a shady pergola walk cooled by sheltering vines. The wide-ranging diversity of monocots, which produce single seed leaves upon germination, is the focus of the adjacent Monocot Garden.

*The Aquatic Garden's graceful formality
is heightened by upright plants that grow
within the pool and on its margins.*

*Monocots like taro, banana, grasses, and grains are a crucial part of the world's food supply. In this garden, their ornamental qualities take center stage with a sensuous display of texture and form.*

## Flower Garden

Facing the grand vista of the Great Lawn, the Flower Garden is the vibrant heart of Wave Hill. Evoking the mellow charm of an English cottage garden, the garden is divided by brick paths and framed by cedar fences reminiscent of those originally installed by the Perkins family. Today, the Flower Garden's adventurous plantings combine vintage and modern perennials, annuals, shrubs, bulbs and tender exotics. Columnar shrubs and container plants add a hint of formality. Rustic arbors, gumdrop yews, and tripods support flowering vines in season and bring winter interest to the garden.

*A changing display of potted plants marks
the garden's central axis. Strolling along
the garden paths offers a variety of
perspectives and moods.*

*Some of the original estate roses, like* 'Mary Wallace' *and* 'New Dawn' *still climb the rustic fence and arbors.* Rosa 'Alchymist' (RIGHT) *is a newer rose bred to resemble an heirloom with its many-petaled, quartered blooms; its yellow, salmon tones did not exist in roses of its type before the twentieth century.*

*This cutleaf Japanese maple, just beyond the garden's western border, adds another striking sculptural element to the landscape.*

# Wave Hill History

Part of New York City's great nineteenth century expansion, today Wave Hill is the only former Hudson River estate that lies within City lines. Wave Hill House was built as a country home in 1843 by jurist William Lewis Morris, and from 1866-1903 was owned by publisher William Henry Appleton. In 1903 George Perkins, a partner of J.P. Morgan, purchased Wave Hill House. Since 1895, Perkins had been accumulating properties along the river – including Oliver Harriman's adjacent villa on the site of what is now Glyndor House. Perkins devoted much of his extraordinary energy to planning the grounds to enhance the property's magnificent vistas. The land was graded and contoured, rare trees and shrubs were planted, and gardens were created to blend harmoniously with the natural beauty of the Hudson River highlands. Many trees, paths and built structures remain while the gardens have evolved around them. Perkins was also instrumental in the inception of the Palisades Interstate Park Commission, which preserved the majestic cliffs across the river from Wave Hill. Throughout its history, Wave Hill House hosted notable guests, among them natural scientists T.H. Huxley and Charles Darwin. Famous tenants included Theodore Roosevelt, Mark Twain, and Arturo Toscanini. Elizabeth, the Queen Mother, visited during the British Delegation's tenancy from 1950-1956.

In 1960, the Perkins-Freeman family deeded Wave Hill to the City of New York. Five years later, Wave Hill was formed as a public garden through a strong community movement. Wave Hill is now one of thirty-four City-owned cultural institutions.

*Mark Twain leased the estate from 1901–1903,*

*setting up a treehouse parlor in the branches of a chestnut*

*tree on the lawn. Of winter at Wave Hill he wrote,*

*"I believe we have the noblest roaring blasts here I have ever*

*known on land; they sing their hoarse song through the big tree*

*tops with splendid energy that thrills me and stirs me and*

*uplifts me makes me want to live always."*

# Index of Selected Plants

PAGE *Plant Name* (Common name, if applicable)

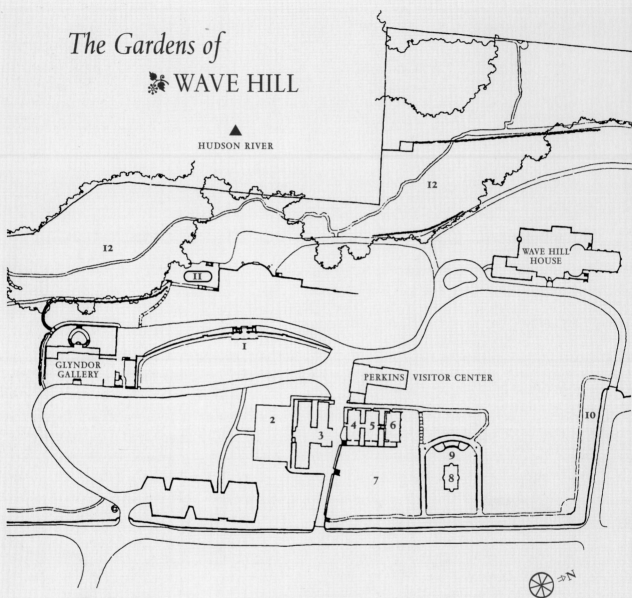

# The Gardens of
## 🌰 WAVE HILL

HUDSON RIVER

12

12

WAVE HILL
HOUSE

II

GLYNDOR
GALLERY

I

PERKINS VISITOR CENTER

2

3

4  5  6

10

7

9

8

N

1. Pergola Overlook

2. Flower Garden

3. Marco Polo Stufano Conservatory

4. Herb Garden

5. Dry Garden

6. T. H. Everett Alpine House

7. Wild Garden

8. Aquatic Garden

9. Monocot Garden

10. Shade Border

11. Elliptical Garden

12. Herbert and Hyonja Abrons Woodland